London

The 'B' type of bus of 1910, the first reliable motor bus produced, can be seen at the London Transport Collection, Syon Park

London

Jeanne Streatfeild

**Mills & Boon
ON
LOCATION
Book no. 14**

Photographs and drawings by
Alec Davis

*The Sherlock Holmes pub, Northum-
berland Street, where 'relics' of the
great detective can be seen*

MILLS & BOON Limited, London

First published in Great Britain 1976
by Mills & Boon Limited, 17 – 19
Foley Street, London W1A 1DR.

© Jeanne Streatfeild 1976

ISBN 0 263.06111.6 (cased)
ISBN 0 263.06112.4 (limp)

Acknowledgements

The publishers are grateful to the
following for permission to reproduce
illustrations:

British Library Board (p. 16); British
Museum (p. 10 – 11); London Transport (p. i); Mansell Collection (pp 44,
61, 63); Museum of London (p. 12 –
13); National Gallery, London (p. 31);
Public Record Office, London (p. 23);
Science Museum, London (p. 74); Sir
John Soane's Museum, London (p. 62
– 3); Victoria & Albert Museum, London (pp. 42 – 3, 58); Zoological Society
of London (pp. 95, 96).

Typeset in IBM Press Roman by
Reproduction Drawings Ltd.

Printed in Great Britain by
Thomson Litho Limited,
East Kilbride, Scotland

Contents

Preface

The aim of this book is to help you understand something of the past two thousand years of London's history. It is not just another guide. Like all the books in the *On Location* series it is designed to encourage you to look and to understand the things you see.

Trooper of the Household Cavalry

If you are a child born in London, there are many pieces of London's past that you pass every day without really noticing. If you are a visitor, then there is much to see for the first time.

But whether you live in London or not, I hope that this book helps you to look, to see — and to understand.

January 1976   *J.S.*

1 Roman London

At the time of Christ, the British Isles were on the very edge of the known world. And although the Romans came to Britain twice under Julius Caesar, in 55 BC and 54 BC, they did not stay. However, in AD 43 they came to settle and to join the 'tin islands' (as the British Isles were called) to the Roman state. Because they came to conquer and to settle it is not surprising that their military headquarters gradually grew into settlements and then into small towns.

But why did the Romans settle by the Thames? Why did they choose to build Londinium at all? The site had several advantages. There were two hills, Ludhill and Cornhill, which were defensively strong; the river Thames was narrow enough to be bridged; and sea-going galleys could use the river, so giving easy communication to the rest of the Empire. (It's difficult to understand how good the choice of site was — for the hills are now covered with tall buildings. If you can, walk up the hill from Blackfriars to St Paul's. It is surprisingly long and steep!)

What do we know about the Romans? We know that they were great architects and road builders. We also know that they were served by a strong army and were easily the strongest country in Europe for the best part of five hundred years.

When the Romans conquered an area they brought peace — and in peaceful conditions trade and crafts could flourish. But because they were conquerors they needed to be able to maintain control of the country they had invaded, and thus roads had to be built.

Roads from Roman London went to every part of the province:
Watling Street went north to St Albans and Chester and south to Dover.
Stane Street went to Chichester.
Ermine Street went to Lincoln.

Along these roads were milestones and boundary marks. You can find a boundary mark in the wall of the Bank of China, Cannon Street. Some experts believe that this is the *lapis millaris* that was originally in the centre of Roman London in the Forum, the point from which all measurements to and from Londinium were taken. Do you know which point is used to calculate mileages from London today?

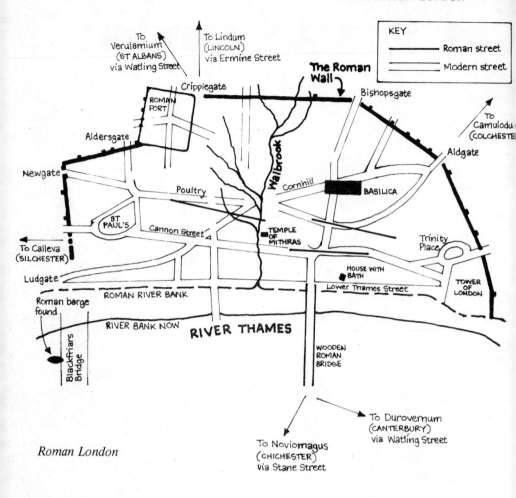

Roman London

The Romans' skill as road builders made for easier communication, which in turn encouraged trade. The settlements along the roads grew into good-sized towns. In them people lived and died and, as generations passed, left behind a whole range of domestic and military relics that are still being discovered today.

Remains of the wall of London at Coopers' Row – the base is Roman, the rest medieval (opposite)

The best evidence of a Roman settlement in London is the wall. Look for remains at:

The bastion at the base of the Wardrobe Tower, Tower of London.

The bastion in the churchyard of St Giles, Cripplegate.

Base of medieval wall outside Tower Hill tube station.

Coopers' Row.

St Alphage churchyard.

Noble Street.

Warwick Lane.

Any section of this wall is worth studying. Look at the base of the wall. What do you notice about the bricks? Are the bricks smaller or larger than the ones we use today? What do you think they are made from? What other material has been incorporated into the wall? How is the wall shaped and held together?

Where London Wall (the name of a street) now runs there was once a Roman fort. You can see the West Gate and a model of this fort (in the new Museum of London).

Although the buildings in this part of London are mostly modern, see how many reminders of its Roman past you can discover: for example, the plaque to show the site of Cripplegate — one of the six gates of the Roman wall. Names like 'Roman House' and 'Barbican' — which means an outer fortification resembling a gatehouse.

Archaeologists have managed to uncover much of Roman London. You can see a large model of the remains of a tessellated pavement in the crypt of All Hallows church, which means you have to go below street level — to the level of Roman London. Does this tell you something about the way man builds upon remains of previous settlements?

The houses of the rich, and public buildings, were often decorated with beautiful mosaics. Like all mosaics, the one illustrated here is made from tiny pieces of fired clay. These pieces are called tesserae. Could you make a design like this, using tiny scraps of paper or even postage stamps?

Roman mosaic — a frieze of dolphins

We know the Romans used tiles for
floor coverings and for roofing, as
well as for water pipes (or conduits).
Many of these have been found and
can be seen in the London museums.
Try to find five different types. Sketch
and note what they have been used
for.

Can you find a tile that has been
marked in any way — perhaps by the
potter who made it, or an animal that
strayed across the clay while it was
still wet? In the Museum of London is
a tile that has the following words on
it: *'Austalis dibis XIII Vagatur sibi
cotidim'* (Austalis has been wandering
off by himself for thirteen days). No
one knows who wrote it — possibly
his workmate who was fed up with
the extra workload!

Christianity did not become the
official religion of the Roman Empire
until AD 380. Until then the Romans
worshipped many gods and goddesses.

*Head of Mithras, the mysterious Persian
sun-god worshipped by the Romans in
the second and third centuries AD*

At a time when there was no radio
and television, no daily papers or
weekly magazines, how do you think
religious ideas spread across the
Empire?

The remains of a Roman temple —
dedicated to Mithras — can still be
visited. Draw a plan of what remains.
The head of Mithras and other valuable
findings are to be seen in the new
Museum of London.

In your visits to the museums you will
have noticed many other aspects of
Roman life. Choose one of the
following and collect photographs and
drawings so that you can compare
similar objects used by Londoners
who came after.
Roman dress — fasteners, pins,
  jewellery.
Roman pots, bottles and kitchenware.
Roman sculpture.
Roman toys.
Roman weapons.

Remember to include on your
drawings a note of the object you have
drawn, where it was originally found
and the period that it dates from. This
will mean that you will have reliable
information to include in any study
you may make later on 'London
through the Ages'.

The Romans finally left Britain in
AD 410, although their influence
remained for several centuries more.

London in the third century AD

2 Saxon London

Little is known of London in Saxon times, but it seems that these tall, fair-haired invaders allowed Roman London to fall into ruins. They even stole the tiles and the stones to use for their own buildings (though these were not grand like those of Rome)! They were warrior farmers and therefore settled in outlying districts such as Padd*ington*, Is*lington*, and *Ham*pstead. These are all Saxon words: 'ton' — a large farm or village; 'ing' — of; and 'ham' — home. Thus Padd-ing-ton is the home of Pad. How many other Saxon place names can you discover in London?

There is little left of early Saxon building because their houses were largely built of wood and thatch, but you can see the foundations of a timber-framed hut in the new Museum of London.

As Christianity spread through southern Britain after the arrival of St Augustine in AD 597, churches began to be built. The foundations of many of London's city churches are Saxon — and include St Bride's, St Paul's and, according to legend, Westminster Abbey. The night before the Abbey was to be consecrated a ferryman rowed a mysterious

A scramasax — a dagger carried by the fierce invaders from northern Europe — in the Tower of London

passenger across the river Thames in his boat. While waiting for his passenger, he suddenly looked up and saw the Abbey alight. The stranger, on his return, revealed his identity as St Peter and told the ferryman that the church had already been consecrated and, providing one tenth of the catch was given to the church and that there was no fishing on Sundays, the Thames would always be filled with salmon.

There are no salmon in the Thames today — but more and more fresh-water fish are being netted between Battersea Bridge and Tower Bridge. What does the legend tell us about the Thames in Saxon times — and what does the return of roach, dace, carp and gudgeon tell us about the river Thames today?

But to return to the Saxon churches . . . the church of All Hallows Berkying-by-the-Tower is the

building that gives us the most clues.
The crypt contains the remains of
the Saxon church. Here you will see a
beautifully carved stone cross.

It is important to remember that few
people could read or write in Saxon
times. It was the monks who were the
teachers and scribes, and it is their
beautiful manuscripts that tell us much
about their way of life. In the British
Museum you can see some of these
manuscripts. Ask to see the Lindisfarne gospels, Beowulf and the Anglo-
Saxon Chronicle.

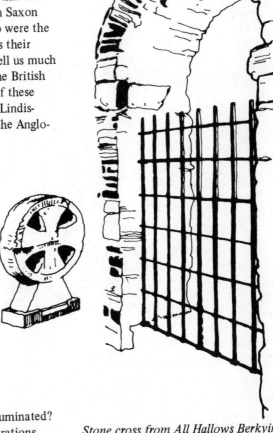

Why are the manuscripts illuminated?
Do you think that the illustrations
would help you understand the story
any better? If you find these illustrations particularly interesting, try to
illuminate a letter yourself. Use
cartridge paper, mapping pens and a
range of coloured inks. Choose a
closed letter for your first attempt (an
O, D, P, B) as these are easier to work.

*Stone cross from All Hallows Berkying-
by-the-Tower and the remains of a
seventh-century arch – probably the
oldest in London – near the entrance
to the crypt of All Hallows*

*The beginning of St Matthew's Gospel
illuminated at Lindisfarne in AD 698*

If the pen and ink work is successful,
try illuminating letters in water
colours using a very fine squirrel or
oxear hair brush. When you are really
competent you might try to decorate
a verse of your favourite poem.

While in the British Museum visit the
Sutton Hoo treasure, a magnificent
collection of armour, bowls, spoons,
an iron standard and beautiful orna-
ments and jewellery. This was all
found in the burial ship of an Anglo-
Saxon chieftain, discovered in Suffolk
in 1939. Although it was not found
in London, the collection tells us
something about the Saxons who
lived in and around the ruins of the
Roman city.

The shrine of Edward the Confessor,
Westminster Abbey

The Saxons settled in the British Isles and, setting up their own kingdoms, lived fairly peacefully. But new invaders came across the channel – the Danes, Vikings or Norsemen. The Danes – like the Saxons before them – saw Britain as a place in which to make their homes. The result was a struggle between Saxon and Dane.

Under Alfred the Great peace was temporarily restored. But to keep the peace Alfred had to make sure his towns could be defended. He rebuilt the walls around London so that the city once more became a centre of trade and of great political importance. It was also the site of many battles between the Saxons and the Danes. You can see the grappling irons used by the Danes for attacking London Bridge in the Museum of London and the Cuming Museum, Southwark. Does this help you understand the nursery rhyme 'London Bridge is falling down'? Finally in 1016 London made an honourable peace with the Danes and their short reign is remembered in place names like St Clement Danes, Greenwich and Aldwych ('Wic' is a Danish word for a temporary camp.)

This period also saw the rebuilding of Westminster Abbey by Edward the Confessor. Edward was the last of the true Saxon kings and the best remembered and loved of Saxon Londoners. Remains of the Saxon Abbey can be seen in the passage leading to the Little Cloister, and in the base of the pillars and walls of the Sanctuary.

When you visit the Abbey find King Edward's tomb. Edward was regarded as a saint and down the centuries many pilgrims visited his shrine. Look at the base of the shrine – the stones have been worked away by the knees of praying pilgrims.

3 Norman London

In 1066 Edward the Confessor died and Harold, his chosen successor, was defeated at Hastings by an army of Norman knights. Their leader was William, Duke of Normandy, known as 'the Conqueror'.

Having taken England by force he built some two hundred motte and bailey castles all over England (see *On Location: Castles*). Each castle was within a day's march of its nearest neighbour — so the country was tightly controlled. He divided the land between his barons who, in return, provided him with fighting men. Land given on these terms was known as a 'fief' from the Latin *feudum* (hence the term 'feudalism').

In the corner of Roman Londinium, William built the Tower. He chose this site to protect the land and river approaches to London. It also had the effect of frightening the citizens. The White Tower is built of stone brought from Caen, the capital of the Duchy of Normandy.

Try to find a reason for stone being brought from Normandy to London (historians offer a number of suggestions). When you are visiting the White Tower try to record the things that interest you by making sketches, writing notes, taking photographs and even recording the Yeoman Warders as they take visitors round the Tower. If you are drawing take a board to rest on, an eraser and a pencil sharpener (the sort that stores the shavings).

Note:
1 The shape of the White Tower.
2 The motte — the White Tower is built on an artificially raised mound of earth.
3 The massively thick walls. Try to discover why they are so solid. (The walls are 4.5 metres thick at the base and 3.5 metres at the top.) How thick are the walls of a modern house?
4 The spiral staircase. Find as many reasons as you can for this design. If you imagine being pushed by an enemy up the stairs would you have a better chance with spiral stairs than if the stairs were straight? Does it matter which way the spiral turns? Would this be true for everyone?
5 The rounded arches, both inside and outside the Tower. Do you think it is easier to build a pointed arch or a rounded one? Which arch

The Tower of London

Features of a pillar

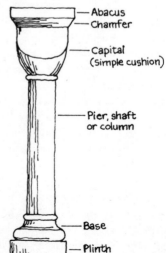

did earlier builders use? Norman
architecture is called 'Romanesque'.
Does this give you a clue?

6 The windows. Some windows have
   narrow slits – others larger openings
   with glass. Which do you think are
   the original windows? On which
   level of the Tower would you expect
   to have wider openings? Why?

7 Pillars and capitals. How does the
   decoration on the capitals vary?

Round arches, St John's Chapel, Tower of London

8 The towers. Which one is a different shape? The Royal Observatory was here until it was moved to Greenwich in 1675 (see pages 49 – 50, 69).
9 The well — which was an essential part of any castle.

The Normans also built beautiful monasteries, abbeys and cathedrals all over England. London still has several magnificent Norman churches. Here are a few particularly interesting ones you could visit:
St Bartholomew the Great, Smithfield.
St John's Chapel, White Tower.
Crypt of St Mary le Bow, Cheapside.
Crypt of St John's Priory, Clerkenwell.
Temple Church (interesting Norman transitional — use of pointed arch).

*Nave of St Bartholomew the Great,
Smithfield (note the Tudor oriel
window, see p. 39)*

*(Opposite) Extract from Domesday
Book, which can be seen at the Public
Record Office and Museum in Chancery
Lane – can you recognize any of
the words?*

This programme of building required
vast sums of money. For this reason
William I ordered Doomsday or Domesday Book (1086) to be compiled, in
which the wealth of each farm was
recorded and tax levied. (The citizens
of London were excluded from the
survey.) It was hoped that this record
would be of value until the day of
judgement, that is Doomsday.

MIDELSEXE.

In Iseldone tenent canonici s̄ pauli .p. v. hid̄ se
defendebat sep̄. Tra. ē .iiii. car̄. Ibi sunt .iii. car̄.
⁊ dim̄. ⁊ adhuc dim̄ poteʃt fieri. Ibi .iiii. uillī ⁊ iiii.
bord̄. Silua .c.l̄. porc̄. ⁊ xx. sol̄. de herbagia.
In totis ualentiis ualet .iiii. lib̄. q̄do recep̄. similit̄.
T.R.E. .c. sol̄. hoc t̄ra iacuit ⁊ iacet in dn̄io s̄ pauli.

Ad s̄c̄m pancratiū tenent canonici s̄ pauli .iiii.
hid̄. Tra ē .ii. car̄. Villā h̄r̄ .i. car̄. ⁊ alia car̄ poteʃt
fieri. Nem̄ ad sepes. Pasta ad pecun̄. ⁊ xx. den̄. Ibi
iiii. uillī q̄ tenent hanc t̄ra sub canon̄. ⁊ vii. cot̄.
In totis ualentiis. ual̄. xl. sol̄. q̄do recep̄. similit̄.
T.R.E. lx. sol̄. hoc t̄ra fuit ⁊ eʃt in dn̄io s̄ pauli.

In Tuifordone h̄r̄ canon̄ s̄ pauli. ii. hid̄. Tra .i. car̄.
⁊ dim̄. Ibi ē .i. car̄. ⁊ dim̄ poteʃt fieri. Ibi .iii. uillī
de .i. virḡ. Pasta ad pecun̄ uill̄. h̄ t̄ra ual̄ ⁊ ualuit
xl. sol̄. h̄ t̄ra ⁊ iacet in dn̄io eccl̄e s̄ pauli.

In ead̄ uilla h̄r̄ ipsi canon̄. ii. h̄. Tra ē .ii. car̄.
⁊ dim̄. ⁊ tant̄ ibi. ⁊ m̄ sunt. Ibi .iiii. uillī q̄ tenent sub
canon̄ hanc t̄ra. ⁊ iiii. bord̄. ⁊ xiii. cot̄. h̄ t̄ra ualet
lx. sol̄. q̄do recep̄. similit̄. T.R.E. xl. sol̄. h̄ eo
iacuit ⁊ iacet in dn̄io eccl̄e s̄ pauli.

In Neutone h̄r̄ canonici s̄ pauli. ii. hid̄. Ad .ii.
car̄. ⁊ dim̄ eʃt ibi t̄ra. ⁊ m̄ sunt. Ibi .iiii. uillī. ⁊ xxvii.
cot̄. de .x. ac̄. h̄ t̄ra ual̄. xl.i. sol̄. q̄do recep̄ similit̄.
T.R.E. xl. sol̄. hec iacuit ⁊ iacet in dn̄io s̄ pauli.

In Hocheʃtone h̄r̄ canon̄ s̄ pauli. .i. hid̄. Tra .i. car̄.
⁊ m̄ ibi eʃt. ⁊ iiii. uillī tenent hanc t̄ra sub canonicis.
Pasta ad pecun̄. h̄ t̄ra ualuit ⁊ ualet xx. sol̄. hec
iacuit ⁊ iacet in dn̄io eccl̄e s̄ pauli.

In Hocheʃtone. tenet canon̄ .p. iii. hid̄. Ad .iii.
car̄ eʃt t̄ra. ⁊ ibi sunt. ⁊ vii. uillī q̄ ten̄ hanc t̄ra.
⁊ xvi. cot̄. In totis ualet .lv. sol̄. q̄do recep̄.
similit̄. T.R.E. lx. sol̄. hoc t̄ iacuit ⁊ iacet
in eccl̄a s̄ pauli.

Canonica s̄ pauli h̄r̄ ad portā epī .x. cot̄.
de .ix. ac̄. q̄ reddit p annū. xviii. sol̄. ⁊ vi. den̄.
T.R.E. similit̄ tenuer̄. ⁊ tant̄ habuer̄.

In Stanestaple h̄r̄ canon̄. iiii. hid̄. Tra ē ad
ii. car̄. ⁊ ibi sunt. ii. ⁊ vii. uillī q̄ ten̄ hanc t̄ra dim̄

s̄ pauli. .i. hid̄. Tra .i. car̄. Ibi ē car̄. ⁊ xxiiii. hoēs
qui reddunt .xxx. sol̄ p annū. h̄ t̄ra iacuit ⁊ iacet
in dn̄io eccl̄e s̄ pauli.

In Osuluestone tenet canon̄ s̄ pauli .p. x. hid̄ se
defend̄. Tra ad .vi. car̄. Ad dn̄m p̄tin̄ .v. hid̄.
⁊ ibi ē. Villī h̄r̄ .v. car̄. Ibi .viii. uillī de .ii. uirḡ.
⁊ vi. bord̄ de .xxx. ac̄. ⁊ ii. cot̄ de .iii. ac̄. ⁊ i. bord̄
de .v. ac̄. Ibi .i. molin̄ de .xii. sol̄. ⁊ v. den̄. p̄
.i. car̄. Pasta ad pec̄ uille. De .i. gurgite. xxx. d̄
In totis ualent̄ ual̄. vi. lib̄. q̄do recep̄ similit̄.
vii. lib̄. hoc t̄ iacuit ⁊ iacet in dn̄io eccl̄e s̄
pauli.

.iiii. TERRA S̄C̄I PETRI WESTMON. [abreuiat]

In villa ubi sedet eccl̄a s̄ PETRI. tenet ab-
loc̄. xiii. hid̄. ⁊ dim̄. Tra ē ad .xi. car̄. Ad
dn̄m p̄tin̄. ix. hide. ⁊ i. uirḡ. ⁊ ibi sunt .iiii. car̄. Villī
car̄. ⁊ i. car̄ plus pot̄ fieri. Ibi .ix. uille q̄ q̄sq̄ de
i. uillī de .i. hida. ⁊ ix. uillī q̄sq̄ de dim̄ uirḡ
de .v. ac̄. ⁊ xl.i. cot̄ q̄ reddit p annū. xl. sol̄. p̄
t̄ra. xi. car̄. Pasta ad pecun̄ uille. Silua
⁊ xx.v. dom̄ militū abbī ⁊ alioz hoīum. qui
viii. sol̄ p annū. In totis ualent̄ ual̄. x. lib̄.
recep̄. similit̄. T.R.E. xii. lib̄. Hoc t̄ fuit
in dn̄io eccl̄e s̄ PETRI. Weʃtmonaʃterii.

In ead̄ uilla ten̄ bainard̄. iii. hid̄ de abbē.
Ad .ii. car̄. ⁊ ibi sunt in dn̄io. ⁊ i. cot̄. Silua .c.
paʃta ad pecun̄. Ibi .iiii. arpenni uinee. m̄
In totis ualent̄ ual̄. lx. sol̄. q̄do recep̄. xx. sol̄.
vii. lib̄. h̄ t̄ra iacuit ⁊ iacet in eccl̄a s̄ petri.

In Hanpeʃtede ten̄ abb̄ s̄ petri. iiii. hid̄. Tra
car̄. Ad dn̄m p̄tin̄. iii. hid̄. ⁊ dim̄. ⁊ ibi ē .i.
h̄r̄. i. car̄. ⁊ alia pot̄ fieri. Ibi .i. uillī de .i. uirḡ.
bord̄ de .i. uirḡ. ⁊ i. serū. Silua .c. porc̄. In t̄
ual̄. l̄. sol̄. q̄do recep̄. simit̄. T.R.E. c. sol̄.

In ead̄ uilla ten̄ Rannulf̄ peuerel sub abbē.
de t̄ra uillan̄. Tra dim̄ car̄. ⁊ ibi ē. h̄ t̄ra
⁊ ual̄. v. sol̄d. hoc t̄ totū simul iacuit ⁊ iacet
eccl̄e s̄ petri. In Spelethorne H[und.]

In Stanes ten̄ abb̄ s̄ petri .p. xix. hid̄

In Norman times the Thames retained its importance in trade. In 1176 the first stone bridge was built across the river. If you visit the Museum of London, you will be able to see a model of this bridge.

Old London Bridge, which took thirty-three years to build and lasted six hundred years, was the only bridge crossing the Thames until 1749

Look at the model:
1 How many arches?
2 How many starlings (boat-like supports between the arches)?
3 Why do you think that the Thames froze above the bridge?
4 Notice the buildings on the bridge: houses, shops and a chapel dedicated to St Thomas of Canterbury.

Thomas à Becket, born in Cheapside,
was Henry II's close friend and was
Archbishop of Canterbury in 1162.
But they quarrelled. The Archbishop
was banned from England, but returned
and was murdered at Canterbury by
four of King Henry's knights. The
bridge was begun in Henry's reign —
and the chapel reminded Londoners of
this.

The importance of the city grew
rapidly, for the Norman kings had
to control not only England but
Normandy (and much of France) too.
But London was well placed to be the
centre of government. It was within
easy reach of France by sea — and
roads from the city spread across the
country. After the death of Henry in
1189, the Exchequer (treasury) moved
from Winchester to London. London
had become the capital city. What do
we mean by this?

4 Medieval London

From 1066 until 1534, when Henry VIII dissolved the monasteries, the church was as powerful as the king. It owned much of the country's land and wealth. Indeed, the importance of a town or city could be measured by the number of churches it contained. London had by far the most in Britain – over one hundred to serve about fifty thousand people. These churches were all within the city wall – an area of about one square mile (2.5 square kilometres).

The architecture of the Middle Ages is called Gothic (can you think why?). It is divided into three periods and is distinguished by its use of the pointed arch. What kind of arch did the Normans use?

Early English, 1190 – 1290 (Westminster Abbey).
Decorated, 1290 – 1377 (St Etheldreda, Holborn).
Perpendicular, 1377 – 1547 (Henry VII Chapel, Westminster Abbey).

If you are interested in the architecture of medieval London visit Westminster Abbey, St Margaret's Westminster and St Stephen's Crypt, Houses of Parliament. This will help you to trace the development of the Gothic style over this long period. Notice how pointed the arches are in the nave and choir of Westminster Abbey compared with those in the Henry VII Chapel. If you enjoy drawing, sketch the differences you discover – or enter them on a simple chart for easy reference (useful for other buildings, too). The questions that follow will help you look for clues, which you can then include in your study.

1 What advantages does the pointed arch have over the rounded arch? Do the pillars still have to be the same distance apart to maintain height?
2 Do the windows become larger or smaller? Why? Compare the dimness of St Bartholomew's with the lightness of the Henry VII Chapel.
3 Look at the 'buttresses'. Compare the thickness of a Norman buttress and an Early English wall. The buttress was an important development. By buttressing, builders could relieve the walls of much of the weight of the stone vaulting. Less weight meant more space for windows.
4 How does the decoration on the capitals vary?
5 How do the shafts change?

Much of everyday life was based upon the churches. Religious houses such as the priory and infirmary at Smithfield (St Bartholomew's) were, in fact, the earliest inns and hospitals. A hospital (from the Latin *hospis,* meaning a 'guest' or 'stranger') was a resting place for pilgrims and travellers and later became a place where the needy were cared for, although not necessarily the sick.

The Hospitallers of St John were founded in the eleventh century and opened a 'hospital' in Jerusalem for pilgrims. They became a military order

Maltese cross – white on black – badge of the Hospitallers of St John. The order was revived in the nineteenth century and you should have no trouble recognizing its members – do you know who they are?

St John's Gate, Clerkenwell

to protect these pilgrims on their way to Jerusalem. In London they built a fine priory, but all that is left today is a Norman crypt and the gatehouse (see page 27).

In medieval times many people made pilgrimages to shrines in England, especially to visit the tomb of Thomas à Becket at Canterbury. The pilgrims told stories to each other during the journey to pass the time. Geoffrey Chaucer recorded these stories in the *Canterbury Tales*.

Westminster Abbey
Pilgrims came to London to visit the shrine of Edward the Confessor in Westminster Abbey. Nearby are many fine medieval royal tombs. Find the plainest of these tombs. This belongs to Edward I, who subdued the Scots and captured the Stone of Scone. It has been suggested that the reason why the tomb is so plain was to comply with his last wishes to his son, that, should the Scots rebel, his flesh was to be boiled and his bones carried before the English army.

Edward I had a coronation chair made in 1301 to contain the famous Stone of Scone. This is the chair on which for almost seven hundred years all our kings and queens have been crowned (two exceptions — Edward V, the boy prince murdered in 1483; Edward VIII, abdicated in 1936). Notice the initials carved on the chair. It was unguarded and the

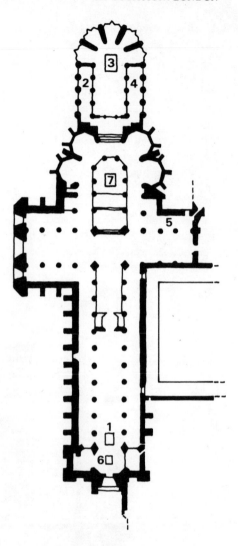

Important tombs in Westminster Abbey
1 Tomb of the Unknown Warrior
2 Tomb of Elizabeth I
3 Tomb of Henry VII and his queen
4 Tomb of Mary Queen of Scots
5 Poets' Corner
6 Memorial to Sir Winston Churchill
7 Tomb of Edward I

boys of Westminster School used to
sneak in at night as a dare and carve
their initials on it. Look for the sword
of Edward III. This weighs 6.8 kg. How
long is it?

Find the tomb of Henry III. He was
a recklessly extravagant king, and
built the greater part of the present-
day Abbey by imposing heavy taxes
on the people. He fell so in debt that

Coronation Chair, Westminster Abbey

Edward III's sword, Westminster Abbey

he was eventually forced to pawn the jewels with which he himself had enriched St Edward's Shrine.

Find the tomb of Richard II. Near the west door there is also a portrait of him — the earliest known portrait of a king. Some say he starved himself to death, but most historians believe that he was murdered.
Of course not all the interesting tombs in Westminster Abbey are medieval. The plan on p. 28 will show you some of the more important ones.

Westminster Hall
Richard II's greatest contribution was the rebuilding of Westminster Hall, which stands before the Thames and the Abbey. Built in 1097 – 9 by William II, it is the oldest and most important part of the medieval Palace of Westminster. The Jewel Tower and St Stephen's Crypt are the only other survivals.

Find:
1 The chained hart badge of Richard II.
2 The statues of kings in niches and window recesses (late fourteenth century).
3 How many bays there are.

What can you discover about the history of Westminster Hall? The chief courts of English Law were here from the late fourteenth century to 1825. Many famous trials have been held here. Among those condemned to death were Sir Thomas More, Bishop

'Giovanni Arnolfini and Giovanna Cenami' by Jan van Eyck

Fisher, Guy Fawkes and seven of his fellow conspirators, and Charles I.

To get an idea of the way people lived in medieval times visit the new Museum of London. It has an outstanding collection of pottery, house furniture, leatherwork, weapons, tools, domestic appliances, jewellery and pilgrim badges.

Paintings give an idea of how the rich and wealthy dressed. The National Gallery and the National Portrait Gallery contain many interesting examples. Go to the Portrait Gallery and see the paintings of medieval kings. A particularly interesting painting is that of the Arnolfini marriage group by Jan van Eyck (1385 – 1441) in the National Gallery. It shows the dress of a wealthy medieval merchant and his wife — a wedding picture. Notice how the bride is dressed in green. (In those days white was the burial colour, brown for the unfortunate ladies over twenty-five, and green for the young and pure.)

Another way of finding out about medieval London is to study the City gilds. These gilds still exist today and are usually known as 'Livery Companies'. People working in the same trade tended to congregate in the same areas, and streets still bear evidence of this, for example Ironmonger Row, Ropemaker Street, Silver Street. What other

Street names – clues to London's past

The Guildhall, centre of government for the City of London for over a thousand years

By the end of medieval times these Livery Companies had become extremely powerful and could prevent any newcomer from practising a trade within the city walls. Although their influence declined in Tudor times, even today they play an important part in the administration of the City of London. The Lord Mayor is always a member of a City Livery Company.

As you wander around the City look for the trade signs of the gilds and the bankers. In the reign of Edward I the Jews, who had been money lenders, were expelled from England and their place taken by the Lombards from Italy. Lombard Street is still a centre of London banking. Wander along it and notice how the banks hang out their signs, just as the medieval money lenders would have done. How many signs can you find? As you make notes remember that they were designed to help people who could neither read nor write!

trade streets can you find? These Livery Companies make a fascinating study. Some will even allow you to visit their magnificent halls – though you often have to make an appointment to do so. There are eighty-two altogether, but the following are known as the Great Twelve.

Mercers	Merchant Taylors
Grocers	Haberdashers
Drapers	Salters
Fishmongers	Ironmongers
Goldsmiths	Vintners
Skinners	Clothworkers

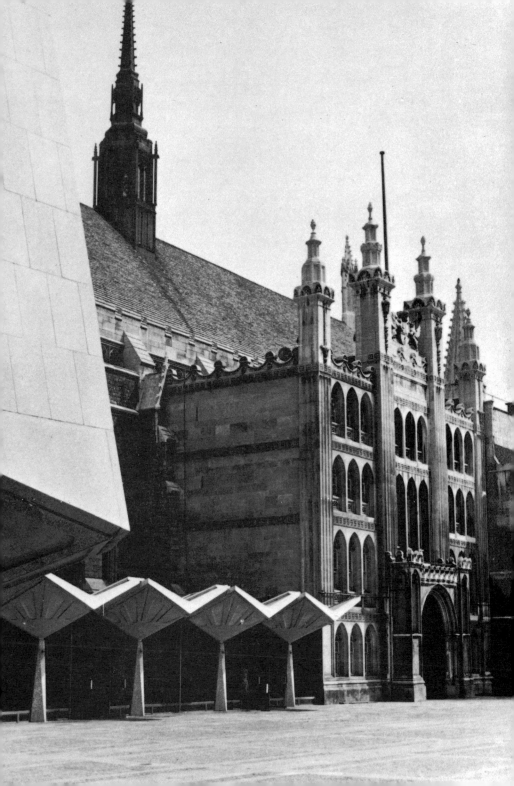

Bank signs in Lombard Street

5 Tudor London

In 1485 Henry Tudor defeated Richard III at the Battle of Bosworth in Leicestershire. He rode to London where he was crowned King Henry VII in Westminster Abbey. Thirty years of civil war had made the country poor and had wiped out many of its aristocratic families. This allowed a new ruling class to appear, a class of traders and merchants. Trade made England rich again — and under Henry VII, Henry VIII and Elizabeth, the nation reached its 'Golden Age'. By 1603, when Elizabeth died, modern England had been born. We can see this slow change happening as we study Tudor London, although early Tudor buildings differed little from those in medieval days.

Tudor Westminster Abbey
The most impressive Perpendicular architecture in London can be seen in the Henry VII Chapel, Westminster Abbey. When you are inside — look up.

Can you see why it is called 'fan vaulting'? Look at the pendants. Each weighs 7 tonnes. (See also the Hampton Court Royal Chapel.)

In how many places can you find the Tudor rose? How many different badges can you discover? They can be best seen on the gates at the entrance to the chapel.

Banners of the Knights of the Order of the Bath, Henry VII Chapel, Westminster Abbey

Look for:
1 The fleurs-de-lis (the emblem of France).
2 The Welsh dragon.
3 The initials HR surmounted by a crown in the bush (can you find out what this refers to?).
4 The leopards of England.
5 The Beaufort portcullis.
6 A falcon – badge of Edward IV.
7 The Tudor rose.

Tudor rose

These armorial symbols occur in many other buildings, on coats of arms and even on uniforms. How long a list can you compile?

The Henry VII Chapel is used for the 'installation' ceremony of the Knights of the Order of the Bath. When a new knight is created his banner is hung and a copper plate engraved with his arms is hammered into his stall – hence he is 'in stalled'. The vergers (the Abbey attendants) are very knowledgeable and helpful and could tell you much about the Order of the Bath and the famous people who have been members. Can you discover where Lord Nelson used to sit? Which is the Sovereign's banner and seat?

From the reign of Henry VII until the death of George II in 1760 this chapel was the main royal burial place. How

Misericord carved as a jester, from the Henry VII Chapel in Westminster Abbey

many Tudor kings and queens can you find buried here? Which Tudor monarch is not buried here?

Tomb effigy of Queen Elizabeth I,
Henry VII Chapel, Westminster Abbey

Hampton Court astronomical clock

Hampton Court Palace

Having seen the tombs of the Tudor
rulers — and perhaps their portraits
in the National Portrait Gallery — try
to visit Hampton Court Palace. Can
you imagine king and court wandering
through the courtyards, visiting the
great kitchen or eating in the fine hall?

Hampton Court was built by Cardinal
Wolsey, a powerful minister of Henry
VIII — who later presented it to his
king. The rich, like Cardinal Wolsey,
entertained lavishly. He kept 500
servants and his palace contained 280
guest rooms.

Notice:
1 This is a palace, not a fortress. How
   do you know?
2 The moat — the last built in
   England — and the crenellations.
3 The palace is built around courtyards rather than facing outwards.
4 The building materials that have
   been used — both inside and outside. How are the bricks laid? Is the
   pattern they make the same as that
   made by bricks laid by modern
   workmen? Can you find any
   diaperwork on the brickwork?
5 The astronomical clock made for
   Henry VIII in 1540 by Nicholas
   Oursian. It is 2.4 metres in diameter
   and shows the hour, date, month,
   number of days since the beginning
   of the year, phases of the moon and
   the time of high water at London
   Bridge. Why do you think it was
   important to know the time of high
   water in Tudor times? What does

this clock tell you about Tudor craftsmanship? Legend has it that when a
resident of the palace dies, the
clock stops.
6 The chimneys. Chimneys were first
   built to carry away smoke. Later,
   however, chimneys were added to a
   building to impress the neighbours.
   How many different patterns can
   you find on the chimney stacks?
7 Windows. Are there any oriel
   windows (projecting bay windows
   usually from an upper storey)? How
   has the glass been fitted into the

Hampton Court oriel window

window frames? What shape is it? How thick is the glass?

8 Ogee arches. How many different kinds of arches can you find? How many ogee arches? What *is* an ogee arch?

St James's Palace and Lambeth Palace are other good examples of Tudor mansions. Is the brickwork similar to that at Hampton Court? Is there any diaper patterning? What happens at the Court of St James today?

But the working Londoner lived in much less impressive houses. Although few remain, we can get an idea of what they looked like by visiting:

Queen's House, Tower of London.
Staple Inn.
Prince Henry's room, Fleet Street.
Gateway to St Bartholomew's.

The spaces in the walls were filled with wattle (upright stakes interwoven with thin branches) and daub (earth, clay or plaster bound with hair or straw), which was then coloured, washed and the timbers coated with tar. Look at the drawing of the Old Curiosity Shop — a good example of seventeenth-century street building. Notice how the house is at right angles to the street. Why does it overhang?

The Old Curiosity Shop, Portsmouth Street

In the Victoria and Albert Museum you will see how a Tudor home was furnished. See how useful the chests were both for storing linen and sitting on. With the addition of a board it became a 'cupboard' for displaying fine tableware — and a drawer transformed it into the earliest chest of drawers. Find the small writing cabinet painted with the royal arms and the devices of Henry VIII and Catherine of Aragon. What wood has been used for the panelling? And you certainly shouldn't miss the Great Bed of Ware! How many do you think could sleep in it?

The English were famous for their wrought silver. In one street alone — the Strand — there are fifty-two goldsmiths' shops. Find the Vyvyan Salt, one of the finest examples of Elizabethan craftsmanship, in the Victoria and Albert Museum. The salt became a very elaborate piece of table decoration, taking on a symbolic role. Those who sat next to the salt were guests of importance. If you were seated a long way away, you might as well go home!

Also in the Victoria and Albert Museum there are some beautiful miniatures. The 'Young man leaning against a tree' by Nicholas Hilliard is very famous.

1 Notice how flamboyantly he is dressed. Men's dress often outshone the women's. Rich cloths were used — silks, velvets, taffetas — embroidered with jewels. What does this tell you about trading in Tudor times?

2 Notice the ruffle — often 22 cm deep — held in place by starch and a wire device known as supportasse or underproper.

3 Why is he so sad? Notice his hand on his heart, the thorny bushes.

Shakespeare's Globe Theatre

Elizabeth I's virginal — what other musical instruments were used in Tudor times?

Find two famous miniatures by Holbein of Miss Pemberton and Anne of Cleves. It was a painting by Holbein of Anne of Cleves that decided Henry VIII to make her his fourth wife — but when he saw her he regretted the decision — he called her 'the Flemish mare'.

The Tudors were funloving and enjoyed entertainment, although you may think that some sports like cock fighting and bear and bull baiting were rather cruel and dangerous. This was also a great period for the theatre — the time of Ben Jonson and William Shakespeare.

Visit Southwark Cathedral and find the memorial to Shakespeare. Look at the modern stained-glass window above it. See how many characters from Shakespeare's plays you can recognize.

Find three other actors and playwrights buried in the choir. One is Shakespeare's brother. Who are the other two?

No matter how gifted you were, to be buried in Westminster Abbey required money and this Ben Jonson did not have. He is said to have remarked jokingly, '6' x 2' is too much for me 2' x 2' will do.' Anyway, he is buried as cheaply as possible — standing up!

Southwark was once the home of the London theatre away from the vigilant eyes of the City Fathers (actors were frowned upon and regarded as low-class citizens). Go to the George Inn, Southwark. You will see a galleried courtyard where plays were performed by strolling companies. Shakespeare's Globe Theatre was in the area and is today remembered by an open-air theatre in the Bear

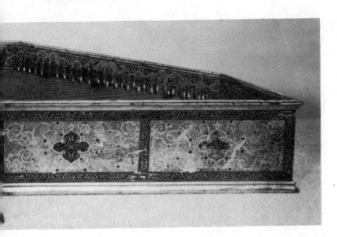

Gardens. In the same road is the Bear
Gardens Museum, which has a
permanent Elizabethan exhibition.
There you can find out more about
the Globe Theatre.

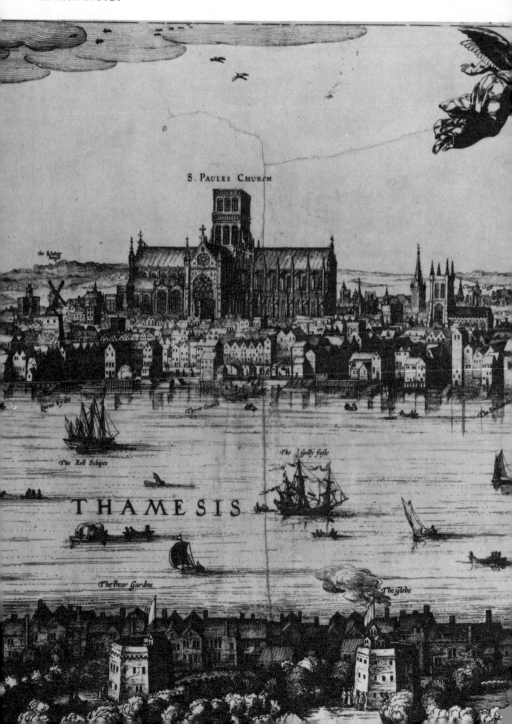

6 Stuart London

Stuart times saw many changes in the
life and face of London. The Plague
and the Great Fire resulted in the
greatest changes, but the Civil War,
the Restoration, the coming of William
and Mary and the growth of
English colonies overseas, had a considerable
effect. Today we are left
with the magnificent churches of
Christopher Wren and the palaces of
Inigo Jones, but remember, at the
beginning of the seventeenth century
London was a place of dirty narrow
streets and wooden houses where only
the bitter winters kept the plague
in check.

The Great Plague of 1665 killed
100,000 people. The bacteria was
spread by fleas who lived on the blood
of the black rat. The houses of those
times, with their strewn rushes, wall
hangings and wooden framework,
provided an ideal breeding and hunting
ground for the rats and their fleas.

The Plague of 1665 was followed by
the Great Fire of 1666. It destroyed
four-fifths of the old city — but it
also destroyed the rat-ridden houses
and gave an opportunity for the city
to be rebuilt. Find an account of the
fire — Samuel Pepys watched it spread
and described it vividly.

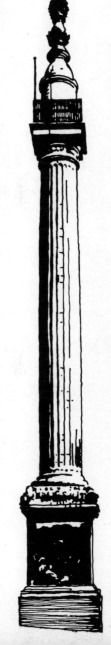

The Monument

St Paul's Church, Covent Garden, by Inigo Jones (1633). The inscription on the pillar on the left reads: 'Near this spot Punch's puppet show was first performed in England and witnessed by Samuel Pepys 1662'

Visit the Monument, built to commemorate the Great Fire of London which started nearby in Pudding Lane. Why is it 202 feet high? Who built it? If you've got the energy, over three hundred steep and spiralling steps will take you to the top for a breathtaking view over London.

After the fire many plans were drawn up for rebuilding a finer new city, but unfortunately haste and private ownership meant that many small lanes and alleyways were re-created, although new laws were passed requiring buildings to be built of brick or stone.

The seventeenth century saw the movement of poorer Londoners towards the east and the richer Londoners to the west, away from the smells of the city which were carried eastwards by the prevailing winds from the west.

In the fashionable West End Inigo Jones introduced the Italian idea of 'piazzas' (squares) at Covent Garden. This was to set a fashion for the next two centuries. Other squares followed quickly such as Lincoln's Inn Fields, St James's Square and Bloomsbury Square. Can you find these squares? How many others can you discover in central London?

Although the Stuart kings lacked the strength and skill of the Tudors, they were great patrons of the arts and have left London with some of its most beautiful buildings. James I was the patron of Inigo Jones, who introduced a new style of architecture based on the classical buildings of Ancient Greece and Rome. It was known as the Palladian style (after Andrea Palladio, an Italian architect). Imagine how strange these buildings must have seemed to Londoners used to buildings of wood and thatch.

When St Paul's was burnt down in the Great Fire, Sir Christopher Wren was asked to produce plans for its rebuilding. Even he had great difficulty persuading the church commissioners to accept his plans for they 'departed too much from the Gothic'. You can see Wren's second model in the Trophy Room, St Paul's, and can walk about inside it. No wonder he cried when this was rejected. The plan finally accepted did not include the huge dome as a central feature, but Sir Christopher was able to modify the design once building had started and build the second largest church dome in the world — no mean achievement!

How long is St Paul's? How high is the
dome? How long did it take to build?
Compare it with the 210 metre length
and 158 metre spire of Old St Paul's.

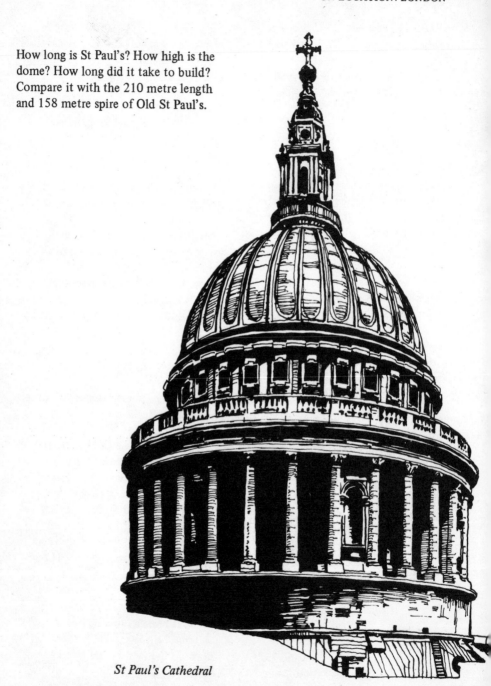

St Paul's Cathedral

Kensington Palace

Can you find John Donne's statue? It is the only one to survive intact from the Great Fire. John Donne was Dean of St Paul's and a great poet and wit. Notice how he is wrapped in a 'shroud' and standing on a funeral urn. This statue was made from a painting of himself that he used to keep under his bed. It may seem slightly odd that he should have dressed up in funeral clothes to have his portrait painted, but, in those days, people liked to remind themselves that death would come — perhaps soon. What else can you find out about John Donne? Can you find any of his poems (one is particularly famous)?

Sir Christopher Wren redesigned fifty-one churches, all highly original and varied in design, as well as giving London three of its most beautiful palaces: Kensington Palace, Greenwich Palace and Hampton Court Palace.

William of Orange suffered from asthma and considered Whitehall too damp — he preferred to live in Kensington Palace. Lord Snowdon and Princess Margaret live here with their family now. Greenwich Palace is now the Royal Naval College. It was a great compliment to Inigo Jones that Christopher Wren built his palace around the Queen's House — pulling down only the Tudor buildings. But when Wren wanted to pull down all the Tudor buildings of Hampton Court, Queen Mary's death (1694) put a stop to his plans.

Try to visit one or more of these buildings.

1 Can you see any similarities between these buildings and St Paul's?
2 What materials are used?
3 Look at the decorations around the capitals.
4 What are the window shapes?
5 How is the building roofed?
6 Look for metal fitments (drains, for example). Are any of them dated?

Doric, Ionic and Corinthian pillars

Armour, clothes and furniture

Londoners have always been very independent from the Crown. During the Civil War they supported Cromwell and the Roundheads. You can see many examples in London of armour and weapons of the Civil War. Visit the Tower, the Wallace Collection and the new Museum of London. What weapons were used?

After the death of Oliver Cromwell in 1658 it was the Londoners who welcomed back Charles II and gladly

turned from their dull puritan ways (as can be seen by studying their clothes and furniture in the new Museum of London, and the Jacobean Room and Costume Court of the Victoria and Albert Museum).

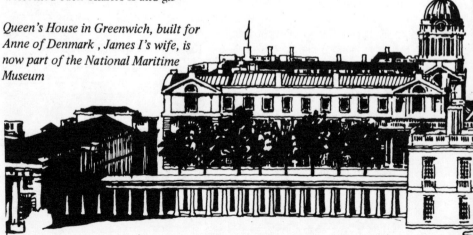

Queen's House in Greenwich, built for Anne of Denmark , James I's wife, is now part of the National Maritime Museum

*Statue of Oliver Cromwell, Old Palace
Yard, Westminster*

St Bride's

St Mary
le Bow

St Clement
Danes

Three Wren churches. There is a story that a baker who saw the steeple of St Bride's, Fleet Street, started the fashion for the tiered wedding cake. St Mary le Bow, Cheapside — true Cockneys are those born within the hearing of the bells of this church. Listen out for the bells of St Clement Danes — there is still a special service during which children are presented with oranges and lemons

Statue of Charles II, Soho Square

CHARLES II
By Caius Gabriel Cibber 1681
Restored by the Square
LADY GILBERT IN 1938

7 Georgian London

In Georgian England travel abroad became fashionable. Indeed no man's education was considered to be complete without the grand tour of southern Europe. In almost everything the influence of the classical can be seen. Go to St Martin-in-the-Fields church. How is it similar to the Parthenon of Athens? Can you recognize the decorations on the capitals, using the information on page 50?

St Martin-in-the-Fields (built by James Gibbs between 1721 and 1726) in Trafalgar Square is one of the best-known churches in London. It is the parish church of the Admiralty and also of the Sovereign. Can you see the royal arms above the portico and the crown on top of the spire? George I was the first church warden (the only King ever to have held such an office) even though he could speak hardly any English.

St Mary-le-Strand — the first of fifty churches that Queen Anne ordered to be built — was completed in 1717. Somerset House, the General Register Office for Births, Marriages and Deaths, is on the right

Another famous church by Gibbs is at the other end of the Strand. It is called St Mary-le-Strand. Why was this street called the Strand? (In Ireland the word 'strand' is still used to mean a beach.)

The increased trade created by the growing Empire brought large fortunes to London's merchants, who built fine houses in the West End. This is also true of cities like Bath and Bristol.

Crewe House in Curzon Street is a fine Georgian town house. However, the squares (mentioned in the last chapter), terraces and crescents are the most characteristic form of Georgian building. Here are some places to see Georgian buildings:

Church Row, Hampstead (one of the finest surviving Georgian streets in London); Doughty Street (you can also visit Charles Dickens's house at No 48); Bedford Square (near British Museum).

1 What do you notice about Georgian houses you have studied?
2 What materials have been used in the building?
3 How many stories high?

Crewe House, Curzon Street

Doughty Street where, at No. 48, Charles Dickens lived (1837 – 9) and wrote Oliver Twist *and* Nicholas Nickleby

4 On which floor do you think the
   main rooms are? Why?
5 How do the windows open? They
   are called sash windows.
6 Which windows are square?
7 What has been used to hide the
   roof – this was a means of main-
   taining the basic rectangular shape.
8 Is the door at ground level?

Sketch a feature of a Georgian house
that interests you (for example,
panelled doorway with its semi-
circular fan-light).

Let's explore further and go inside
one of these houses. You can visit the
houses of two well-known eighteenth-
century personalities. William Hogarth
(his house is in Chiswick) and Dr
Samuel Johnson (his house is at 17
Gough Square, just off Fleet Street).
It was here that Dr Johnson produced
his famous dictionary, first published
in 1755. Can you find an early edition
of his dictionary here?

You might like to find out more about
Dr Johnson for yourselves as he was
one of the most famous people of the
period. He was also a very colourful
character and his writings tell us much
about Georgian London, which he
loved. It was he who said, 'Sir, when a
man is tired of London he is tired of
life; for there is in London all that
life can afford.'

Furniture
Dr Johnson's house was small compared to those of places like St James's

and Mayfair. Unfortunately we cannot
go inside any of these, but in the
Victoria and Albert Museum there is a
room from Henrietta Place (behind
Debenham's, Oxford Street) designed
by James Gibbs (see page 58).

Architects like Kent and Adam were
now concerned with the inside as well
as the outside of a house and also
designed furniture. English craftsmanship during the eighteenth century
reached a level that has rarely been
bettered. A close examination of six
rooms in the Victoria and Albert
Museum (57, 57a, 58, 125, 122, 121)
will give you a clear picture of their
skill in producing jewellery, carpets,
silver, earthenware, china, porcelain,
plasterwork and room decoration,
embroidery, miniatures and furniture.

Do not attempt to study all of these,
but choose one and trace its development through the eighteenth century.
For example, chairs at the beginning
of the period were little more than
stools with arms and backs added.
They were in fact called 'back stools'
What changes do you notice as the
century progresses?

Also visit the Geffrye Museum in Kings-
land Road. The museum was opened
in 1914 in Shoreditch, an area famous
for cabinet making, and has a fine
collection of furniture from Elizabethan times to the present day. The
actual museum buildings were once
almshouses built in 1715, and are a
fine example of early Georgian
architecture.

A Georgian room interior in the Victoria and Albert Museum

(Opposite) Downing Street: at No 10 lives the Prime Minister; at No. 11 the Chancellor of the Exchequer

Sir Robert Walpole

Walpole is sometimes regarded as the first prime minister although he had no such title and his role was very different from that of our prime ministers today. He was given No. 10 Downing Street by George II and in turn presented the house to the nation.

When Queen Caroline, George II's wife, wanted to make Hyde Park once more the private property of the monarch, she asked Sir Robert Walpole what it would cost. He replied, 'Three crowns Madam. The crowns of England, Scotland and Ireland.' (The crown was also a coin worth 5 shillings or 25p.) However, she did manage to have the Serpentine built for the private use of the Royal Family.

In the Victoria and Albert Museum you will find the Walpole Salver. This was made by the London silversmith Paul de Lamerie for Sir Robert Walpole from silver melted down from the Exchequer Seal after the death of George I in 1727.

Fashion

The paintings of William Hogarth, Joshua Reynolds and Thomas Gainsborough in the National and the Tate Galleries will tell you a great deal about eighteenth-century fashion. If you study them carefully they will also tell you much about their way of life.

Eighteenth-century doll's house, Bethnal Green Museum

How long would it take to dress and make-up in the mornings? The basic component of the make-up was lead. Imagine what that would do to the skin! Examples of costumes can be seen in the Victoria and Albert Museum and the Museum of London.

The Bethnal Green Museum is also worth visiting. The toys there will tell you much about eighteenth-century dress and elegant living. In eighteenth-century language a 'toy' was 'a small expensive extravagance'. These toys were set out in a doll's house — a home in miniature — day-beds, chairs, tables, all in their proper styles with all the items to make up the 'tea equipage' — teapot, cream, milk jug, dredgers. Tea would be served with hot buttered muffins.

Coffee houses

A great feature of the period were the coffee houses. Coffee, and more especially tea, was an eighteenth-century craze. Mincing Lane in the City is still the centre of the tea trade. Coffee houses were great meeting places and no doubt Dr Samuel Johnson would frequently have been seen in the ones around Fleet Street with his group of literary friends.

Some of the coffee houses became centres of business and trading — Lloyd's, on the corner of Leadenhall and Lime Street in the City, grew out of a gathering of merchants at a local coffee house. It is now one of the greatest insurance companies in the world. Many relics of Admiral Nelson are kept there, including the logbook that records his famous order: 'England expects . . .' How much can you find out about Lloyd's? Two interesting features are that the tables are still arranged as in a coffee house and the messengers are called 'waiters'. Find out why the Lutine Bell is struck once for news of disaster and twice for good news.

Lloyd's coffee house 1798

Many coffee houses became clubs, like White's, Boodle's, Brook's — all still to be found in St James's Street. But although you can no longer see an eighteenth-century coffee house there are some fine Georgian shops still in existence, for example Fribourg and Treyer in the Haymarket, Hatchards in Piccadilly, and Lock & Co., home of the bowler hat, in St James's.

Poverty, crime and punishment

London attracted many people hoping to make their fortunes, but only the lucky few were to achieve this. Most joined the poor in the tumbledown houses and narrow alleyways of South-wark, Whitechapel and Poplar — to the south and east of the City.

Poverty forced many to crime. The first paid police force, known as the Bow Street Runners, was created by Henry Fielding, a magistrate and author of the famous novel *Tom Jones*. Although the original court house no longer exists, there is still a court there today. It faces Covent Garden Opera House. What can you find out about the Bow Street Runners and the highwayman, Dick Turpin?

Punishments in the eighteenth century were very harsh. You could be hanged for picking pockets if the value of the stolen goods exceeded one shilling (5p). Furthermore, hangings and whippings were regarded as an entertainment, not only for the mob but also for the gentry. Visit the Museum of London to see the Whipping Post.

'Canvassing for Votes' by William Hogarth

What can you find out about the
Tyburn Tree? Its site is today marked
by a plaque set on an island at the
Marble Arch end of Edgware Road.
How do you think the expressions 'in
the cart', 'going west' and 'left in the
lurch' came about? Think how the
prisoners would have travelled. Look
at the position of the Tyburn Tree and
Newgate Jail (now the Old Bailey) on
the map.

Although little remains of the poor
parts of eighteenth-century London,
William Hogarth (often regarded as the
first newspaper cartoonist) gives us a
good idea of the quality of life
enjoyed by the poor in those times.
You can see his paintings and engravings
in Sir John Soane's Museum; the
Thomas Coram Foundation for
Children; the National Gallery and in
his own home in Chiswick.

Eighteenth-century court-room scene

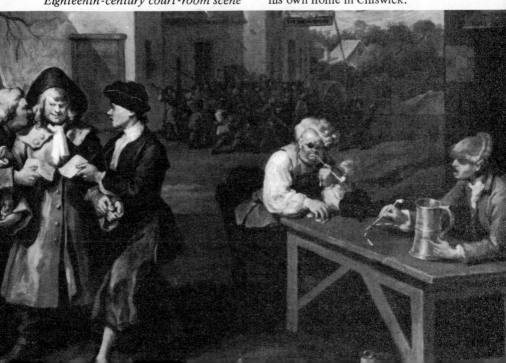

ALL SOULS, LANGHAM PLACE
New Church Complex with Rooms at Rd...

8 Regency London

The Regency period (1811 – 20) is perhaps the most exciting in London's history. Wellington had beaten the French under Napoleon. The Prince Regent wanted to make London as magnificent as Napoleon's Paris. More money was therefore spent on the capital's architecture than at any other time and a great plan for London prepared — and completed.

Even so some of the plans were left unfulfilled. Marble Arch, originally designed by John Nash as the main gateway to Buckingham Palace, stands quite alone. On top there should have been a statue of George IV. A great supporter of the arts and follower of fashion, George IV failed to pay the sculptor, Chantrey. However, the sculptor got his own back. What article of clothing is missing?

John Nash 1752 – 1835
The architect appointed by the Prince Regent to put his dreams into practice was John Nash. Between 1811 and 1835 Nash designed and built the Royal Mile — from Carlton House to Regent's Park.

All Souls, Langham Place, built 1822 – 4. Can you suggest a reason for the unusual shape of this church?

Sadly, apart from Carlton House Terrace and the great mansions of Regent's Park, little remains of Nash's grand route. It's worth while walking along the route to see how many buildings you can find. What very famous streets and circuses were created? A circus was made where there was a slight bend in the route. There is one major bend where Regent Street comes to an end. Here there is no circus. What has been built in its place?

There was a great variety of buildings along Regent Street, but at one section, known as the Quadrant, all the buildings were the same. Is this still true today? How did it get the name 'the Quadrant'? Think of a circle divided into sections.

Duke of York
The Duke of York was the Prince Regent's younger brother. Remember the nursery rhyme:
  The grand old Duke of York
  He had 10,000 men
  He marched them up to the top of
    the hill
  And he marched them down again.
It doesn't exactly flatter him as commander-in-chief of the British Army! In fact he carried out many

reforms. He was often in debt. People said that the reason why he was placed so high on his column in Waterloo Place was so that he would be out of reach of his creditors.

Here are some things to find out about Regency houses.

1   Are these houses similar to the Georgian houses you have studied?

Constitution or Wellington Arch, Hyde Park Corner. The equestrian statue of the Duke of Wellington, which stood on top of the arch from 1845, was removed in 1911 and replaced by the present 'Peace in a Quadriga'

2 How many stories is each building?

3 Are the windows all the same shape and size?

4 How has Nash made these houses look like palaces?

5 What do the houses appear to be made of? (Look at the backs of the houses to see what was actually used.)

6 Why should Nash want to give the impression that his buildings were made of stone? (Think of the ancient classical buildings.)

7 How many different 'classical' influences can you find?

Stucco

This was painted cement made to imitate stone and used by architects of the time because it was cheaper. Great pains were taken to imitate as faithfully as possible the real thing — notice the horizontal and vertical lines to represent stone jointing. Each stone was even 'frescoed' to imitate weathering. When Nash could afford it he used Bath stone — for example, Buckingham Palace and All Souls, Langham Place.

Coade stone

Another form of imitation stone widely used was 'Coade Stone'. The lion shown here has a bottle of beer inside him because he once stood outside a brewery.

Westminster Bridge (the lion is made of Coade stone) and the Houses of Parliament. How can you tell that Parliament is in session?

Sir John Soane (1753 - 1837)
The other outstanding architect of this
period was Sir John Soane, who is best
known for his rebuilding of the Bank
of England. The Bank of England is
the government's banker — where the
gold reserve is kept. How important
do you think security arrangements
are here? Do you think Soane did a
good job? Try going inside — you won't
get very far!

Perhaps more interesting is Soane's
own house, which he gave to the
nation to be opened to the public free
of charge. There are many interesting
things in the house. Look at his
pictures and plans for London and
imagine what it would have been like
if he rather than Nash had been the
King's personal architect. Can you
find the Egyptian sarcophagus? Ask to
see the Hogarth paintings (see page
63). Notice particularly Soane's use
of light. How has he used mirrors and
coloured glass? How has he used 'top
lighting'? What kind of man do you
think he was?

Other places where you can see ex-
amples of Sir John Soane's work are:
Dulwich Picture Gallery and
Mausoleum.
St John's, Bethnal Green.
Holy Trinity, Marylebone. (Because
this is so near to Park Crescent and
Regent's Park, it would be an obvious
choice if you wanted to compare the
work of John Nash and Sir John
Soane.)

National collections
Other important buildings of this
period are our first two national
museums: the British Museum and
the National Gallery.

The British Museum was built by Sir
Robert Smirke between 1823 and
1852. Sir Robert Smirke was a pupil
of Sir John Soane. Look at the portico
of the main entrance. What is the style
of the columns (see page 50)? How
many are there on the main facade?
The British Museum is the largest and
most important of its kind in the
world.

As a place to study the history of art,
the National Gallery (built by William
Wilkins in 1834 - 7) has few equals. Of
particular interest to this period are
the paintings of John Constable (1776
- 1837) and J.M.W. Turner (1775 -
1851).

Admiral Lord Nelson
Trafalgar Square, planned by John
Nash and laid out by Sir Charles Barry
between 1829 and 1841, commemorates
not only Admiral Nelson's great
victory of the Battle of Trafalgar of
1805, but also the Empire, which this
naval power secured.

What other admirals have statues here
and what countries of our former
Empire are represented? The statue of
Lord Nelson is 5.29 metres high,
exactly three times his life size. How
tall was he? Look at the four bronze
reliefs at the base depicting famous

The British Museum

battles won by the great admiral. These, and the lions, cast from an original by Edward Landseer, Queen Victoria's favourite animal painter, were made from naval cannon. (Queen Victoria was very fond of animals — when presented with a list of condemned prisoners on the occasion of her Silver Jubilee, she pardoned all but one who had been cruel to animals.)

The National Maritime Museum was also built to commemorate the Battle of Trafalgar. Note the colonnades on either side of the Queen's House (see page 50 – 1), which now houses the National Maritime Museum. As well as housing relics and personal possessions of Lord Nelson, it has a unique collection of our naval history and the development of the boat. Nelson's tomb, by the way, is in the crypt of St Paul's. It's unusual — whom was it originally designed for?

The Duke of Wellington
The other great military figure of this time was Arthur Wellesley, Duke of Wellington (d. 1852). He is commemorated by the Wellington Arch (see page 66) and a bronze statue at Hyde Park Corner. The 'Iron Duke' is riding

The National Gallery and Nelson's Column

No. 1 London and the Wellington Statue

his favourite horse, Copenhagen, and looking towards his old home, No.1 London. Why do you think it was called No.1? Does this tell you how built up the area west of this point once was?

No.1 London (or Apsley House) is now the Wellington Museum and contains many of the Duke's belongings, including valuable paintings and victory trophies as well as a 4.5 metre statue of Napoleon, his arch enemy. Napoleon refused the statue because the tiny statue of Victory on his palm was facing away from him as though about to take off. The statue was given to Wellington by the Prince Regent.

Fashion
Some changes in fashion that occurred at this time have lasted until today – knickers, nightdresses and trousers were introduced. Once more visit the costume sections of the Victoria and Albert and the new Museum of London to get a more vivid picture of the dress of the time.

What do you notice about the man's coat, shoes, trousers, neckpiece and hat? The men's coats were known as swallow-tails. Can you suggest why? Do you ever see men wearing clothes like this today? Have you ever seen a hunt or a funeral?

What do you notice about the woman's waistline, headgear, shoes and the cut of her dress? The ladies' dresses were almost transparent. What materials do you think they were made of? People

might have bought clothes like this from shops in the Burlington Arcade, built in 1829, the first shopping street of its kind in England. This privately owned arcade still retains much of its Regency flavour. It has its own 'beadles' (policemen) to enforce the law.

Industrial Revolution
This period was also one of invention. In the North and the Midlands the 'industrial revolution' was changing the face of Britain. Coal and iron brought wealth – and dirt and smoke and grime. Visit the Science Museum and see how many important inventors and inventions you can discover.

Transport
London was the market for the goods from these northern industrial areas; better transport was therefore needed than the carts and dirt roads of the eighteenth century.

The Grand Junction Canal was completed in 1805, linking London with the Midlands. Take a barge from Little Venice to London Zoo and imagine how difficult it must have been to build these waterways across Britain. Sadly the canals proved too slow and the inventions of Trevithick, Headley and Stephenson led to the

Burlington Arcade – built 'for the gratification of the publick and to give employment to industrious females'

growth of railways and a new age in
transport. If trains could run quickly
upon rails, then people could live in
the country and work in London. How
do you think that this helped London
to grow?

*Model of Trevithick's locomotive
'Catch-me-who-can', from the Science
Museum (Crown Copyright)*

9 Victorian London

In Victorian times London became the largest city in the world, partly as a result of its position as the capital of a great Empire and partly as a result of the inventiveness of Britain's engineers. The introduction of new building methods and new forms of transport made it possible for London to grow rapidly outwards.

Railways

How did the railways help London to grow? Think of the way people would have travelled to work before the railways were built. The 'railway mania' reached its peak in 1846 and tremendous competition meant that many lines wound their way into the borders of Georgian London. Those coming from the south carried mainly passengers (the first London commuters) and those from the north brought goods. Can you suggest why? Huge goods yards were needed, like those at Chalk Farm. Here you can visit the Round House, now a theatre.

King's Cross and St Pancras

Go and look at King's Cross and St Pancras or any London mainline station. This will give you an idea of the variety of style and materials used by the Victorian builders. King's Cross was built 1851-2 by Lewis Cubitt whose firm is still building today. St Pancras was built by Sir Gilbert Scott 1868-74 — an example of High Victorian Gothic.

When visiting St Pancras look at:
the rounded arches
the pointed arches
the pillars
the parapets
the gables
the chimneys
the towers
the spires
the railings
the ornamentation

Do any of these remind you of earlier periods of architecture? Does this suggest why it is called 'high Victorian Gothic'? Compare this building with the enormous arches and openness of King's Cross. Behind Sir Gilbert Scott's façade you will find the huge iron and glass train shed of W. H. Barlow.

The use of iron and glass revolutionized building techniques. Sadly, the greatest of these buildings, the Crystal Palace built in 1851 to house the Great Exhibition, was burnt down in 1936.

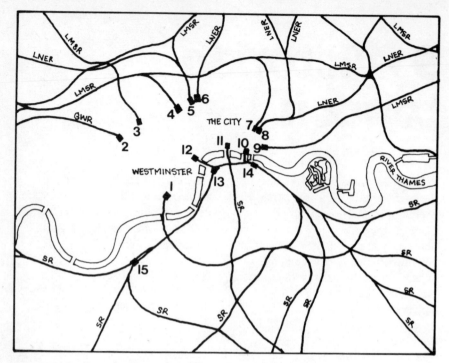

Railway termini of London (before nationalization)

1 Victoria
2 Paddington
3 St Marylebone
4 Euston
5 St Pancras
6 King's Cross
7 Broad Street
8 Liverpool Street
9 Fenchurch Street
10 Cannon Street
11 Holborn Viaduct
12 Charing Cross
13 Waterloo
14 London Bridge
15 Clapham Junction

SR: Southern Railway
GWR: Great Western Railway
LMSR: London, Midland & Scottish Railway
LNER: London & North-Eastern Railway

But one of the earliest of these buildings, the Palm House, Kew Gardens, still survives. Two other buildings in this style are the Floral Hall in Covent Garden Market and Smithfield Market.

These iron and glass buildings were the first form of pre-fabrication and even Paddington Station took only one year to build (in contrast, the Houses of Parliament took fifty-eight.)

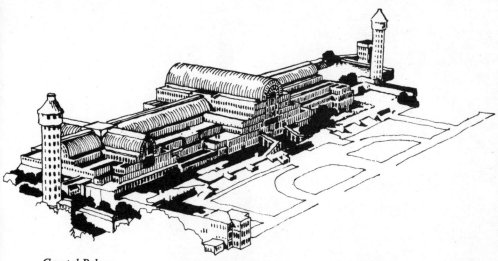

Crystal Palace

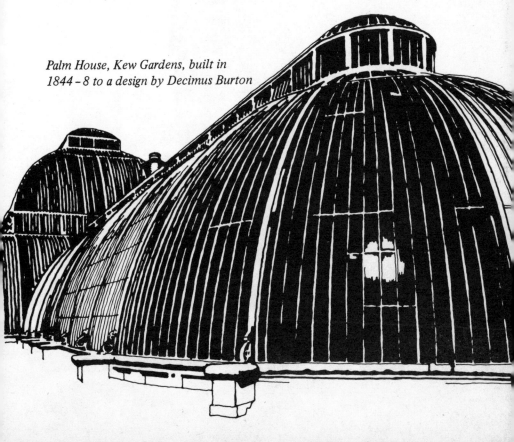

*Palm House, Kew Gardens, built in
1844 – 8 to a design by Decimus Burton*

Prince Albert, Queen Victoria's husband, was a great patron of the arts and is commemorated by the Albert Memorial and the Albert Hall (behind the memorial)

The Law Courts, designed by G. E. Street (1874) in thirteenth-century style. Notice the towers, turrets and pinnacles. What does this remind you of?

Famous buildings

The Victorians were very proud of their parliamentary and legal systems and of their position as a cultural and scientific centre of the world. This is reflected in many of their buildings: the Houses of Parliament, the Law Courts, the Albert Hall and the Albert Memorial.

Built by Sir Charles Barry (1840-88) the Houses of Parliament are thought by many to be the finest Victorian buildings in London. But there were disadvantages. As the Thames was London's main sewer the windows had to be kept closed during debates.

The Albert Memorial was designed by Sir George Gilbert Scott and built between 1863 and 1876. It is worth very close inspection. Can you find out which four continents are represented? How are Agriculture, Commerce, Engineering and Manufacturers shown? Find the epitaph to Prince Albert. What does it say? Does the way it is made remind you of anything you have seen before? What do you think of this memorial?

The book the Prince holds on his knee is a catalogue of the Great Exhibition

for which he was largely responsible.
The profits went to help pay for the
museums along Exhibition Road. These
museums, together with the Bethnal
Green Museum, the new Museum of
London and the London Transport
Collection will provide you with
endless material for further study of
the Victorians. (Talking of museums,
Museums and Galleries in Great Britain
is a very good investment. Published
by ABC Travel Guides Ltd, it devotes
sixteen pages to London.)

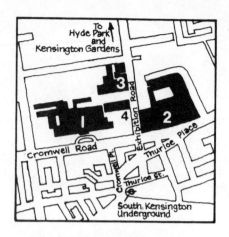

1 *Natural History Museum*
2 *Victoria and Albert Museum*
3 *Science Museum*
4 *Geological Museum*

Theatres
The Palace Theatre, Shaftesbury
Avenue, and the Covent Garden Opera
House reflect the tastes of Victorian
theatre goers. Queen Victoria loved
opera. Fashionable society went either

*Royal Opera House portico, Covent
Garden*

to Covent Garden, built in 1858, or to Her Majesty's in the Haymarket. The ordinary people preferred the music hall. This is reflected in the lack of important playwrights until the end of the century. The best known are Gilbert and Sullivan with their popular operas, often portraying London life of the time. Richard D'Oyly Carte built the Palace Theatre and the Savoy Hotel with the money he made from mounting the operas of Gilbert and Sullivan.

Tower Bridge

Tower Bridge was built between 1886 and 1894. Each section of roadway (called a bascule) weighs about 1,000 tonnes. Look at the footway across the top. This is now closed because it was such a popular place for suicides.

The docks

Downstream from Tower Bridge the river Thames is lined with warehouses and docks. Behind these there are rows of terraced houses and small factories. This was the main industrial quarter of London in the nineteenth century. You

Tower Bridge — the last bridge between the Pool of London and the open sea

can still see much of it by taking a
boat from Westminster Pier or Tower
Pier to Greenwich. At Greenwich visit
the *Cutty Sark* and the National
Maritime Museum (see pages 50 and
69).

Just as the *Cutty Sark* (launched in
1869) was quickly eclipsed by steam
ships, so the docks of this part of the
Thames have outlived their use. Today
they are a ghostly reminder of their
Victorian past.

Houses rich and poor
Bombing and bulldozing have left few
houses of the Victorian poor for us to
see, although examples can still be
found in such areas as the East End,
Willesden and Camberwell. Towards
the end of Victoria's reign, benefactors
like George Peabody built blocks of
'model' dwellings for the poor. Many
Peabody buildings can still be seen
near Covent Garden and Drury Lane,
around the Elephant and Castle and to
the north of the City and the Barbican.

Public services
The Victorians introduced education
for everbody and in 1876 brought in
a law preventing any child under ten
from gaining employment. Many of
the red-brick schools, three or four
stories high, with separate boys' and
girls' entrances, still exist today. How
do these schools compare with the
school you attend? If you go to a

school like the one described, look
for clues to the past – dates on iron-
work and brickwork, the remains of
gas lighting. Has your headteacher an
old log book he can show you?

Lighting, sewerage systems and public
transport were developed rapidly
towards the end of the period. The

*No. 58 Knightsbridge – formerly the
home of Hudson the Railway King,
now the French Embassy*

gas lamp shown opposite is in
Regent's Park. Can you find any
others? Victorian public toilets are
often interesting architecturally.
Those in Star Yard, Holborn, are still
in use and are an example of cast-iron
prefabrication.

The sewerage, drains and underground
were often built side by side. The
Victoria Embankment was constructed
so that a major sewerage drain and the
Metropolitan and District Line could
be built underneath. London had the
world's first underground railway —
started in 1863. It linked Paddington
to King's Cross and Farringdon Street.
Why do you think this was the first
line to be built? Travel along the line.
Which stations do you go through?

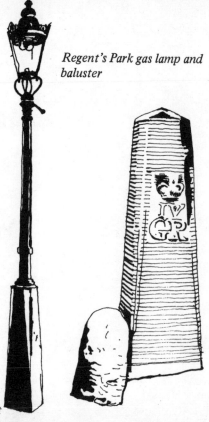

Regent's Park gas lamp and baluster

James Smith & Sons, 53 New Oxford Street

How near the surface is the track? Can
you think why there are so many
parts where the track is open to the
sky?

Many Victorians were very wealthy,
and shops were an important feature
of life. The shop shown here is
Victorian and sells swordsticks,
ceremonial maces and horsewhips, as
well as umbrellas. It is well worth a
visit. Another book in this series — *On
Location: Shops and Markets* — will
help you find out more about this
subject if it is something that interests
you.

Much money was also spent building
churches. All over London there are
Victorian churches, for as the town
expanded churches were built to serve
the new estates. There is Brompton
Oratory (1884, Italian Baroque), St
Giles, Camberwell (1844, Early
Decorated by Sir George Gilbert Scott),
and St George's, Southwark (1848,
Decorated Gothic by Pugin). However,
the most important is the Roman
Catholic cathedral at Westminster.
Made of brick striped with cream paint,
and built mainly in 1895 - 1905, it is
an example of Victorian revivalist
architecture — Byzantine.

During Queen Victoria's reign the
population of London quadrupled
to over six and a half million people.
It was necessary to house all these
people. The railways, underground,

Westminster Cathedral

omnibuses and trams made it possible for people to live further from their work and so suburbia came into existence, first in places like Camberwell, Paddington and Islington, then later in more rural areas like Lewisham, Willesden and Tottenham.

The Victorian age can be summed up by the Victoria Memorial standing outside Buckingham Palace. It has figures representing Truth, Motherhood and Justice, Science and Art, Naval and Military power, Peace and Progress, Industry and Agriculture. And at the top Victory, Courage and Constancy. At its centre sits the great Queen who dominated the age.

The Mall: a processional way laid out as a national memorial to Queen Victoria.

1   Buckingham Palace
2   Queen Victoria Memorial and Gardens
3   Lancaster House
4   Clarence House
5   St James's Palace
6   Marlborough House
7   Duke of York's column
8   Admiralty Arch
9   Ministry of Defence
10 Home and Foreign Office
11 Treasury and Department of the Environment

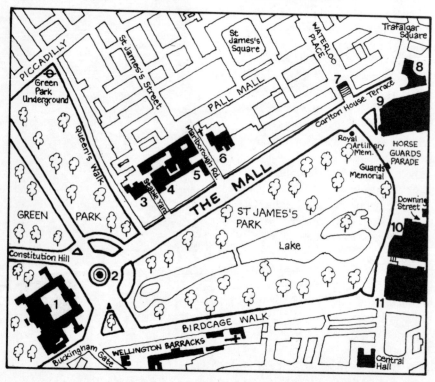

10 Modern London

In the twentieth century London continued to grow rapidly outwards into new surburban areas like Wembley, Twickenham, Orpington and St Mary le Cray. At the same time new housing estates were built in central London such as Dolphin Square (1936), Churchill Gardens (1950s) and the Barbican (1970s). Dolphin Square claims to have the largest number of flats in one block in the world. Being near to Westminster it is popular for MPs. The Barbican has the tallest flats in England. How many stories high are they?

For a long time it was thought that tall buildings could not be built on the soft London clay. However, re-inforced concrete and modern building methods have caused the London skyline to change dramatically since the war. Among the best known of the skyscrapers are the Post Office Tower (1965), BP Building (1966), Centrepoint (1965), the Shell Building (1962), the Millbank Tower (1963) and the new Stock Exchange (1972). Can you find out what they are used for? They illustrate London's continued importance as a centre of communication, government, commerce and trade.

The Shell Building is at the heart of the South Bank complex. This was first developed as the site of the Festival of Britain (1951), the centenary of the Great Exhibition.

One of the most successful examples of modern architecture in London is the Royal Festival Hall. More recently, downstream, the Queen Elizabeth Hall, the Hayward Gallery, the National Film Theatre and the New National Theatre have been built.

London remains a great centre of art; visit the Bayswater Road or Piccadilly at the weekend and go to the Tate Gallery to see the contrasts of modern art and London life.

In many parts of London you can see examples of modern sculpture. Among the best known are 'Locking Piece' – on the Embankment near the Tate Gallery – and 'Knife Edge-Two Piece' – by the Jewel Tower, Westminster.

Shops, of course, play an increasingly important part in the lives of Londoners. Peter Jones, for its steel-framed 1930s exterior, should be visited, as should the lively and noisy pedestrians-only Carnaby Street. Others, parti-

cularly the department stores, have
become household names. Places like
Harrod's and Fortnum and Mason's
have a museum-like appeal with their
high standard of display and service.

Millbank Tower, 118 metres high;
the Tate Gallery is on the left

'Zemran' by William Pye, presented to the GLC by Nadia Nerina

The Post Office Tower – 175 metres high with a 12-metre mast – the tallest building in Britain

Transport

Just as rail transport revolutionized the nineteenth century, the petrol engine has revolutionized road and air transport in the twentieth century. Major roads now snake their way into central London and many underpasses and flyovers have been built, for example Hyde Park Corner underpass and the Brent Cross flyover.

But even the roads and railways cannot cope with rush-hour traffic and so new underground lines are being built. The Victoria Line (1968-71) is the most modern in the world, and the first to be built in central London since 1949. A new line, the Fleet, is under construction. Can you find out which places this line will link? Why is it called the Fleet?

London Bridge, once the oldest and only bridge across the Thames, is now the newest – completed in 1974. How many bridges are there now? Are any of them particularly interesting? The piers of Blackfriars Bridge, for example, were built in the form of church pulpits in memory of the Dominican friars whose church once stood on the north bank. A good way of seeing London is to take a motor-boat ride – upstream to Kew, downstream to Greenwich – from Westminster Pier.

Royal Festival Hall, South Bank

London is a great centre of international air traffic, and the observation tower at London Airport is the best place from which to see modern jets taking off and landing. There is much to find out about at the airport — types of aircraft, destinations, flying times, frequency of air traffic and so on.

The City
In two thousand years of history London has seen sweeping changes, but the City remains the historic core and centre of London's business life. Today its streets throng with people only during office hours. At evenings and weekends it remains deserted.

However, life is being brought back. Wander round the Barbican, by St Paul's. Here houses and flats, schools, shops, pubs and restaurants are being built. The new Museum of London, the Royal Shakespeare Company and the London Symphony Orchestra are to move here. Perhaps people will once more travel into the City for entertainment. Remember the meaning of 'Barbican' (see page 10)? Here in the midst of modern London we can still see the wall built by the Romans, the founders of our great capital.

11 Some things to do

There are many ways in which you could record your explorations in London. Perhaps the most difficult decision to make is that of choice — what aspects of London do you wish to record and how do you wish to record them? Is your account to consist entirely of your own photographs or your own drawings? Do you wish to restrict yourself to one period of history (for example Tudor London), to one particular topic (for example Statues in London), or to one particular area (for example the City of London)?

Having chosen a theme, you will also need to decide how best to present your findings and to classify them in an attractive and easily readable way. The following suggestions are meant only as a guide, but they do indicate the sort of approach you could attempt.

Scrapbook or loose-leaf folder? Loose-leaf folders are the most satisfactory methods of keeping material. You can continually add information on new sheets to expand a section and rewrite sheets should you make mistakes. Loose-leaf folders can be made to any shape and size — but a scrapbook tends to become somewhat unwieldy if it becomes too thick. Another advantage of the folder is that you can change the colour of the paper according to the topic you are considering — churches on red paper, for example, museums on blue, street names on yellow, plaques and wall inscriptions on grey. On the other hand, scrapbooks are ideal if you are keeping a diary-type record (for example when visiting London for a short holiday or on a field trip).

Whatever method you choose, mount your material with care. Adequate space should be left round each piece, so that every page has a pattern of its own. Remember that only a small amount of paste is necessary to hold each piece in position. If you think that you might want to rearrange a page later on, use Cow gum or rubber paste. These adhesives allow papers to be peeled apart, undamaged, even after a considerable passage of time.

Lettering needs to be done with care. Unless your lettering is of high quality, do your titles on paper and mount them in your book when they are dry. Bamboo-tipped pens are probably the easiest to use for this, although the softer felt tips are almost as good.

As your knowledge of London increases you may wish to try to present your findings in a less conventional way than those already suggested. The following might appeal to you:

1 People in London
Select a famous person and try to discover how much of his London remains, for example Christopher Wren, George Handel, Samuel Pepys, John Evelyn. Try to include extracts from their writings and drawings and photographs of buildings they knew.

2 Walks in London
Throughout this book I have suggested short walks that will help you to understand particular building styles. Instead of a diary-type account, make a collection of your own illustrated maps of London.

3 London's River
Take a short length of London's river (for example from Lambeth Bridge to Waterloo Bridge) and record in detail the interesting buildings along it.

4 Customs and ceremonies of London
As you explore London you will learn something of the peculiar customs of the capital. What is a Pearly Queen, where are the Queen's Keys paraded nightly, when are the cellars of the Houses of Parliament searched for explosives, when and why do the watermen race for a coat and badge, where can you find Gresham's grasshopper?

Kipling House, Villiers Street

5   London at work

The various markets of London are
worthy of study. How much can you
discover about Leadenhall, Poultry,
Smithfield, Old Covent Garden,
Billingsgate?

6   London's transport

Apart from the many railway stations,
there is the underground railway to
explore, London airport, the river (by
hydrofoil) two cross-river tunnels, a
free ferry and numerous working
canals. If you are very resourceful you
will find a toll road too. Visit the
London Transport Collection in Syon
Park.

7   Signs and Plaques

London is rich in odd street names,
house plaques (which tell of famous
folk who once lived in the house) —
and even shops whose sign boards tell
of unusual things once sold within.

*The Embankment and four interesting
ships (left to right):*
Discovery: *Captain Scott's polar
research ship*
HMS Wellington: *premises of the
Master Mariners, the only City Livery
Company to own a floating hall*
HMS Chrysanthemum: *naval training
ship*
HMS President: *naval training ship*

8   Bygones

In any large city that has developed
over the centuries you will discover
oddments left over from a previous
age — hexagonal pillar boxes, gas lamps
converted to electricity, the doorway
to a ducal palace, a Roman inscription,
a stone slab commemorating a gibbet
or a notorious prison.

Yeoman and Chelsea Pensioner – make a study of the interesting uniforms to be seen in London

9 Changing London

No city ever stops still and things are being built or pulled down all the time. You could make this your study. Why was it necessary for the old Covent Garden, for instance, to move elsewhere? What do you think should be done with the old buildings?

Bath time at London Zoo

10 London at play

And if you're tired of walking round hot, dusty streets, there are plenty of other things for you to do. Parks, gardens, boat trips, swimming baths, the zoo – just some of the ways you can enjoy yourself in London.

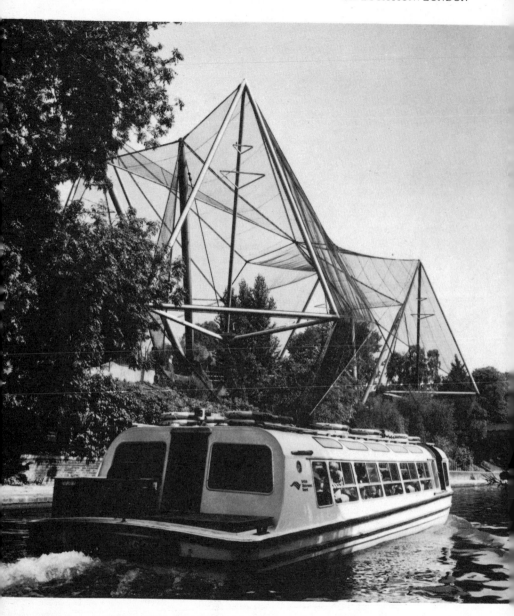

On a boat trip from Little Venice to Regent's Park and the Zoo you will see this peculiar metal construction – what is it?